Table of Contents

Executive Summary

Our national security depends on our ability to share the right information, with the right people, at the right time. This information sharing mandate requires sustained and responsible collaboration between Federal, state, local, tribal, territorial, private sector, and foreign partners. Over the last few years, we have successfully streamlined policies and processes, overcome cultural barriers, and better integrated information systems to enable information sharing. Today's dynamic operating environment, however, challenges us to continue improving information sharing and safeguarding processes and capabilities. While innovation has enhanced our ability to share, increased sharing has created the potential for vulnerabilities requiring strengthened safeguarding practices. The 2012 *National Strategy for Information Sharing and Safeguarding* provides guidance for effective development, integration, and implementation of policies, processes, standards, and technologies to promote secure and responsible information sharing.

Our responses to these challenges must be strategic and grounded in three core principles. First, in treating *Information as a National Asset,* we recognize departments and agencies have achieved an unprecedented ability to gather, store, and use information consistent with their missions and applicable legal authorities; correspondingly they have an obligation to make that information available to support national security missions. Second, our approach recognizes *Information Sharing and Safeguarding Requires Shared Risk Management.* In order to build and sustain the trust required to share with one another, we must work together to identify and collectively reduce risk, rather than avoiding information loss by not sharing at all. Third, the core premise *Information Informs Decisionmaking* underlies all our actions and reminds us better decisionmaking is the purpose of sharing information in the first place. The *Strategy* focuses on achieving five goals:

1. **Drive Collective Action through Collaboration and Accountability.** We can best reach our shared vision when working together, using governance models that enable mission achievement, adopting common processes where possible to build trust, simplifying the information sharing agreement development process, and supporting efforts through performance management, training, and incentives.

2. **Improve Information Discovery and Access through Common Standards.** Improving discovery and access involves developing clear policies for making information available to approved individuals. Secure discovery and access relies on identity, authentication, and authorization controls, data tagging, enterprise-wide data correlation, common information sharing standards, and a rigorous process to certify and validate their use.

3. **Optimize Mission Effectiveness through Shared Services and Interoperability.** Efforts to optimize mission effectiveness include shared services, data and network interoperability, and increased efficiency in acquisition.

4. **Strengthen Information Safeguarding through Structural Reform, Policy, and Technical Solutions.** To foster trust and safeguard our information, policies and coordinating bodies must focus on identifying, preventing, and mitigating insider threats and external intrusions, while

departments and agencies work to enhance capabilities for data-level controls, automated monitoring, and cross-classification solutions.

5. **Protect Privacy, Civil Rights, and Civil Liberties through Consistency and Compliance.** Integral to maintaining the public trust is increasing the consistency by which we apply privacy, civil rights, and civil liberties protections across the government, building corresponding safeguards into the development of information sharing operations, and promoting accountability and compliance mechanisms.

As we execute the *Strategy* together, we will harness our collective resolve to treat information as a national asset, make it discoverable and retrievable by all authorized users, and arm those charged with preserving the security of our Nation. Only as we work together, hold ourselves accountable, and take concerted ownership of advancing our goals, will we achieve the safety and success our country rightfully demands and fully deserves.

I. Introduction

To prevent acts of terrorism on American soil, we must enlist all of our intelligence, law enforcement, and homeland security capabilities. We will continue to integrate and leverage state and major urban area fusion centers that have the capability to share classified information; establish a nationwide framework for reporting suspicious activity; and implement an integrated approach to our counterterrorism information systems to ensure that the analysts, agents, and officers who protect us have access to all relevant intelligence throughout the government. We are improving information sharing and cooperation by linking networks to facilitate Federal, state, and local capabilities to seamlessly exchange messages and information, conduct searches, and collaborate.

– National Security Strategy, May 2010

Our national security relies on our ability to share the right information, with the right people, at the right time. As the world becomes an increasingly networked place, addressing the challenges to national security—foreign and domestic—requires sustained collaboration and responsible information sharing. The imperative to secure and protect the American public is a partnership shared at all levels including Federal, state, local, tribal, and territorial. Partnerships and collaboration must occur within and among intelligence, defense, diplomatic, homeland security, law enforcement, and private sector communities.

Scope

Anchored on the 2010 *National Security Strategy*, the 2012 *National Strategy for Information Sharing and Safeguarding* (hereafter referred to as the *Strategy*) provides guidance for more effective integration and implementation of policies, processes, standards, and technologies to promote secure and responsible national security information sharing.

The *Strategy* does not define particular categories or types of information that must be shared. Rather, it shifts the focus of information sharing and safeguarding policy to defining information requirements that support effective decisionmaking. The *Strategy* outlines a vision with a national policy roadmap to guide information sharing and safeguarding within existing law and policy. This *Strategy* does not replace the *National Strategy for Information Sharing* (2007 NSIS), as the 2007 NSIS continues to provide a policy framework and directs many core initiatives intended to improve information sharing. This *Strategy* will continue to highlight appropriate protection of individual rights—privacy and civil liberties are most relevant in this context. Nonetheless, departments and agencies must never lose sight of their responsibility to protect the civil rights of all Americans in accordance with their respective authorities.

Vision

It is a national priority to efficiently, effectively, and appropriately share and safeguard information so any authorized individual (Federal, state, local, tribal, territorial, private sector or foreign partner) can prevent harm to the American people and protect national security. The Strategy points toward a future in which information supports national security decisionmaking by providing the right information, at any time, to any authorized user, restricted only by law or policy, not technology; and where safeguarding measures, to include a comprehensive regimen of accountability, prevent the misuse of the information.

Building on Success

While the 2012 *Strategy* establishes goals for the future, the 2007 NSIS continues to provide the policy framework for institutionalizing requirements of the *Intelligence Reform and Terrorism Prevention Act of 2004*, specifically to improve integration and responsible information sharing related to terrorism, homeland security, and weapons of mass destruction. The 2007 NSIS also highlights the importance of gathering and reporting locally generated information while emphasizing two-way flows of timely and actionable information among government, public, and private entities. To date, the concerted efforts of these partners have resulted in significant progress.

- Established a National Network of Fusion Centers owned and managed by state and local entities, which use the Nationwide Suspicious Activity Reporting (SAR) Initiative (NSI) to share terrorism information among all levels of government; and with consistent policies to protect individual privacy, civil rights, and civil liberties. There have been increasing levels of collaboration among the fusion centers, the Federal Bureau of Investigation's (FBI) Joint Terrorism Task Forces, Field and Regional Intelligence Groups, Federal, state, and local law enforcement agencies, High Intensity Drug Trafficking Area programs, Regional Information Sharing System centers, intelligence and crime analysis units, and via initiatives like the Fusion Liaison Officer Program, which includes tribal and non-law enforcement partners.

- Adopted the National Information Exchange Model (NIEM), a successful example of a common way to structure data exchanges to better enable information sharing. NIEM is now used by many Federal agencies, State governments, private sector organizations, and foreign partners. As a side benefit, NIEM promotes information technology (IT) industry adoption as a result of partnering with standards development organizations (SDOs).

- Established a plan to unify and align user identification and authentication on systems, through the Federal Identity Credential and Access Management (FICAM) framework under the *National Strategy for Trusted Identities in Cyberspace*. This represents a critical step toward establishing individual accountability and facilitating the appropriate level of information access.

- Provided access to multiple data repositories across departments and agencies, consistent with mission authorities and legal protections. For example, analysts at the National Counterterrorism Center (NCTC) now have access to over 30 Federal networks containing terrorism information. This profoundly contrasts the pre-9/11 environment characterized by agency-centric data repositories.

- Developed a single authoritative database of known or suspected international terrorist identities at NCTC. Pertinent information from NCTC's database now can be exported to the FBI's Terrorist Screening Center database, which also includes domestic known or reasonably suspected terrorist identities, a marked improvement to the previous multiple, non-integrated lists.

- Enhanced communications to facilitate dialogue between departments and agencies and with other partners. For example, the FBI and Department of Homeland Security (DHS), augmented by the Interagency Threat Assessment and Coordination Group, hold classified video teleconferences three times a day, 365 days a year, with over a dozen Federal counterterrorism entities. Products of these efforts are available, as appropriate, to non-Federal partners.

Through these foundational efforts, we have successfully begun to streamline policies and processes, overcome cultural barriers, improve IT system interoperability, and enable pertinent information sharing.

II. The Operating Environment

Ongoing advances in information technology challenge stakeholders to identify and implement information management best practices. While innovation allows information to move unimpeded across jurisdictional, functional, and organizational boundaries, increased information sharing may create vulnerabilities that expose us to compromise, exploitation, manipulation, and unauthorized use of that information. These issues often point to challenges in governance, information management, and resourcing.

- **Threats to national security remain diverse.** Terrorist attacks on the homeland and U.S. interests abroad; insider threats to information systems; nuclear proliferation; cyber attacks; global economic pressures; and regional instabilities are a few examples of the diverse threats we face. Future threats will only continue to evolve as our adversaries learn to counter our security measures. This wide-ranging and dynamic array of challenges illustrates the range of need for timely and effective information sharing and safeguarding.

- **Unaligned management practices and policies present obstacles.** Departments and agencies need to recognize their statutory responsibilities for sharing and safeguarding information, overcome historically insular practices and policies, embrace a government-wide perspective, and agree to participate in structured collaboration. Better coordinated management frameworks will provide a mechanism for creating policies and processes that enable responsible information sharing and safeguarding in an efficient and cost-effective manner.

- **Quality control of shared information is a challenge.** Information to support national security may be incomplete, vague, or inaccurate. Building tools and techniques that help stakeholders to assess the provenance of information when acquired, accessed, retained, reproduced, used, managed, shared, and safeguarded is essential for ensuring quality control.

- **Valid constraints on sharing information exist.** There will always be some restrictions on sharing sensitive operational, law enforcement, or personally identifiable information. In addition, foreign partners, State governments, and the private sector may impose limits on use or dissemination of their information. Efforts that respect these realities and provide a responsible means to share information, such as "tagging" data, identifying and authenticating users, and securing networks, are critical to appropriately protecting this information.

- **A lack of network interoperability creates barriers across departments and agencies and missions.** Differences in policies and technologies prevent authorized users from gaining access to critical resources and information on disparate networks. Efforts are underway to enable interoperability for users accessing information within "sensitive but unclassified" and classified networks, while maintaining high levels of protection for that information.

- **Increased information sharing demands advanced correlation and analytic capabilities.** Turning an abundance of data into actionable information or intelligence remains an enduring problem. Many initiatives are underway, however, to enable information correlation with advanced analytics, including new tools, techniques, and training.

- **Efficiency is a necessity.** The economic downturn of the past several years has affected everyone, including households, businesses, and governments. Mission objectives must be met with innovation and agility in an extremely austere budget environment.

- **Improperly safeguarded information is a liability.** Our ability to properly protect information as it is shared is directly related to the maturity of governance processes, access controls, identity management, enterprise audit capabilities, and network interoperability efforts. This takes us from controlling quality and access within individual networks and systems to sharing information management across stakeholders.

III. Principles

The ideas, values, energy, creativity, and resilience of our citizens are America's greatest resource. We will support the development of prepared, vigilant, and engaged communities and underscore that our citizens are the heart of a resilient country. And we must tap the ingenuity outside government through strategic partnerships with the private sector, nongovernmental organizations, foundations, and community-based organizations. Such partnerships are critical to U.S. success at home and abroad, and we will support them through enhanced opportunities for engagement, coordination, transparency, and information sharing.

– National Security Strategy, May 2010

To accomplish the *Strategy's* vision, efforts are grounded in three core principles.

1. Information as a National Asset

Departments and agencies have achieved an unprecedented ability to gather, store, and use information consistent with their missions and applicable legal authorities. They have corresponding obligations to make information available to any agency, department, or partner with a relevant national security mission and to manage that information in a manner that is lawful and protects individual rights. This requires a continued maturation of information security, access, and safeguarding policies and processes.

For example, building an enterprise-wide approach moves stakeholders away from agency-specific networks and applications and provides secure and authorized access to information in ways that allow information sharing across departments and agencies.

Managing information as a national asset simultaneously demands stakeholders make it available to those who need it, while also keeping it secure from unauthorized or unintended use. While originators are accountable for the accuracy, characterization, and availability of shared information, consumers who use it for reporting or decision making equally share responsibility and accountability for its manner of use. In short, information collected, analyzed, and disseminated by every stakeholder must be discoverable and retrievable, consistent with necessary legal restrictions, and guided by government-wide policies, standards, and management frameworks.

2. Information Sharing and Safeguarding Requires Shared Risk Management

Building trust in sharing and safeguarding requires the ability to manage rather than avoid risk. Risk to national security increases when the approach to sharing is inconsistent, fragmented, or managed from a single-agency perspective. Risk decreases, however, with sound policies and standards, increased awareness and comprehensive training, effective governance, and enhanced accountability. Performance management and compliance monitoring at the enterprise level will aid governance, inform decisions, and help foster a culture that emphasizes the importance of responsible sharing.

Sharing and safeguarding are not mutually exclusive. Policies, practices, and methods for information sharing and safeguarding can enable appropriate confidentiality while increasing transparency. To realize the benefits of sharing information, stakeholders mitigate and manage risk by taking appropriate measures to build trust in the processes that safeguard information from compromise. As the mission imperative for sharing increases, so too does the need to improve interoperable safeguarding techniques.

3. Information Informs Decisionmaking

Informed decisionmaking requires the ability to discover, retrieve, and use accurate, relevant, timely, and actionable information. Likewise, our national security depends upon an ability to make information easily accessible to Federal, state, local, tribal, territorial, private sector, and foreign partners in a trusted manner, given the appropriate mission context. The objective is to increase the usefulness of information in operations through the consistent application of policies, guidelines, exchange standards, and common frameworks, while always respecting privacy and individual rights.

Ultimately, the value of responsible information sharing is measured by its contribution to proactive decision making. The above principles and below goals will help us achieve an environment wherein decisions are driven by information that reflects our best assessments at every level—from frontline personnel to agency heads.

IV. Goals

1. Drive Collective Action through Collaboration and Accountability

1.1 Improve Governance to Promote Collaboration

Governance plays a critical role in setting priorities and driving decisions. The bodies charged with these responsibilities, along with performance and compliance monitoring, exist at all echelons of government. Enabling their work demands clear, harmonized, and complementary charters that support collaboration and policy enforcement at the lowest possible level, yet still allow elevation of issues through the White House policy process. An effective governance structure accounts for the complexities of a diverse range of missions, acknowledges resource realities, reduces gaps, minimizes redundancies, and aligns stakeholder policy development and implementation.

1.2 Increase the Use of Common Processes

Many communities use common processes for acquiring, accessing, retaining, producing, using, managing, sharing, and safeguarding information. The SAR process used by the National Network of Fusion Centers and local law enforcement entities, for example, includes stakeholder outreach, privacy protections, training, and enabling technology to identify and report suspicious activity in jurisdictions across the country, and serves as the unified focal point for sharing SAR information. Common processes, like SAR, provide organizations a template for repeatable, interoperable, and trusted protocols. Standardization, with built-in flexibility for evolving mission requirements, also improves timely information discovery, access, and exchange and makes it easier to integrate new partners into existing information flows. Not only does increasing the use of common processes provide opportunities to strengthen privacy, civil rights, and civil liberties, it enables the implementation of vetted measures to safeguard information.

1.3 Streamline the Development of Information Sharing Agreements

Information sharing to protect national security relies on availability of information from many government agencies, the private sector, and foreign partners, all of which have diverse missions and information collection and dissemination policies. As a result, developing interagency information sharing agreements is often a critical step in the success of cross-agency collaboration. Unfortunately, this step is often protracted as agencies attempt to determine mutually agreeable requirements and restrictions related to information access, handling, and use based on differing missions, requirements, restrictions, and authorities. Creating a template, based on common legal and policy compliance requirements would streamline the process, facilitate issue resolution, and enhance partnerships with private sector and foreign partners.

1.4 Encourage Progress through Performance Management, Training, and Incentives

Achieving the goals of this *Strategy* requires a management approach that includes incentives for performance at both the organizational and individual levels. Departments and agencies benefit from integrating their performance management approaches to support a holistic view of progress towards achieving information sharing and safeguarding goals. Stakeholders should not only measure improvements in information sharing and safeguarding processes (e.g., discoverability, timeliness, accuracy, compliance, and oversight), but also measure their overall effectiveness (e.g., how shared information helps to achieve the mission). Performance management and metrics, when paired with effective leadership, reinforces progress and motivates personnel to meet high expectations and professional standards. Investing in staff through training and incentives also helps foster a culture that values information sharing and safeguarding, extending to organizations beyond our immediate communities.

2. Improve Information Discovery and Access through Common Standards

2.1 Develop Clear Policies for Discovery and Access

A central intent of information sharing is to make certain information is both discoverable and accessible by those with a legitimate need, in a timely manner. Discovery and access are distinct concepts: the first addresses a user's ability to identify the existence of information, and the second relates to a user's ability to retrieve it. Our national security demands relevant information is made discoverable, in accordance with existing laws and policies, to appropriate personnel. Discovery and access require clear and consistent policy and standards, as well as technical guidance for implementing interoperable processes and technology.

2.2 Improve Identity, Authentication, and Authorization Controls

Information discovery requires a standardized approach to authentication so participating entities can validate and trust the identities of users attempting to log into their systems. Information holders have often created their own authentication services resulting in users requiring unique credentials for accessing different systems or networks. Using trusted, interoperable authentication services will minimize the number of required credentials, drive out unnecessary anonymity, and achieve efficiencies by eliminating stand-alone authentication services.

Once user identities are authenticated, their unique attributes assist in determining if access to information is authorized. Both information originators and consumers share responsibility for using standard processes, attributes, and "rules of use" to support authentication and authorization decisions. Further, user attributes require dynamic management to inform these decisions, including provisions for agile updates and removal of user access. Greater policy and technical alignment across departments and agencies will enable implementation of interoperable capabilities that engender confidence and trust in the process of confirming appropriate users while also providing access to mission-relevant information.

2.3 Promote Data-Level Tagging

Most information authorization models are limited to access controls defined and enforced at the network or application-level, rather than at the data-level using inherent characteristics of specific information resources. As networks are consolidated and shared services are adopted, access controls must be applied on the data itself, using "tags." Information tagging is an approach where standard attributes—tags—are attached to a piece of information to describe it. While manual discovery and access capabilities benefit from information tagging by guiding users directly to specific information based on their profile, it also can enable automated enforcement of access decisions based on mission-relevance. By matching the user attributes with corresponding information attributes, the automated delivery of mission-specific information is improved along with the security and protection of that information from inappropriate recipients. Information tagging further assists in meeting records management requirements, responding to disclosure inquiries, integrating privacy protections, and remediating erroneous data disclosures and modifications.

2.4 Enhance Enterprise-Wide Data Correlation

Connecting related information from disparate department and agency databases can mean the difference between identifying a threat during the planning stage or analyzing what could have been done to thwart the attack after it occurs. Data correlation and advanced analytics, coupled with integrated sharing and safeguarding protections, will enable users to reference authoritative, up-to-date information across multiple agency holdings. This capability can support analysts' efforts to identify relationships among people, places, things, and characteristics that are otherwise not apparent. To advance this capability while taking into account increasing volumes of information, stakeholders need to make their information accessible so an analyst can create a single query to search across many information sources. Analysts also need automated capabilities to establish linkages across holdings and generate alerts when mission-relevant information becomes available. While current technologies require centralized information repositories, which may yet remain appropriate in some limited cases, a decentralized approach allows the originator to maintain and update information as needed. This promises increased speed in sharing and higher levels of information fidelity. Successful data correlation also requires a validation component to determine the veracity and applicability of information before action.

2.5 Drive the Use of Information Sharing Standards

Meeting the mission need for enterprise-wide discovery and access warrants the use of standards. By reusing existing standards, stakeholders can benefit from the time, resources, and experience invested by others to fully vet and implement a new standard. As a result, capabilities to meet mission needs can be more rapidly, efficiently, and effectively applied without developing ad-hoc custom solutions or unique standards for single use. Prudent information sharing leverages the use of voluntary consensus standards, as described in existing Federal policy, wherein government uses standards created by established SDOs, which often incorporate government, industry, and international membership. With this approach, we first aim to adopt existing standards to meet mission needs, and when none are available, use SDOs to address the gap.

2.6 Support Enterprise-Wide Certification and Conformance

Given the abundance of standards available throughout the government, the private sector, and the international community, decisionmakers and users are faced with the challenge of determining which standard is most appropriate to satisfy their requirements while also supporting interoperability with other partners. Consequently, there is a need for a process to validate, certify, and require the interoperability of technology solutions used to share and safeguard information. This, in turn, will help inform decisionmakers of the most appropriate standards to employ while also sending a clear signal to industry which standards to use in developing tools and products that advance interoperability and support a broader set of mission needs.

3. Optimize Mission Effectiveness through Shared Services and Interoperability

3.1 Share Services that Benefit All Partners

Across the government, departments and agencies have begun to embrace a shared computing model, sometimes referred to as "cloud computing." In this model, data centers are consolidated and computer infrastructures are employed as a shared service. Hosting systems and applications on common infra-structures distributes workload, reduces requirements for computing capacity, and lowers total cost. The future promises to bring additional enhancements by offering capabilities beyond shared computing, such as shared application and shared information services. As a result, departments and agencies can adopt existing capabilities and focus on developing the services and technologies that best align with their mission and expertise. In particular, shared capabilities will allow departments and agencies to better deliver targeted services to specific end-users, as opposed to trying to serve all classes of users with all required capabilities. The projected advantages of this approach include streamlined cost and efficiency, as well as the opportunity to reduce the number of unique interfaces and required standards.

3.2 Improve Assured Data, Services, and Network Interoperability

While the shared service model offers significant enhancements, it does not guarantee interoperability or improved information sharing. Departments and agencies continue to wrestle with the challenge of using legacy data, services and systems that have varying degrees of connectivity across and among various classified and unclassified networks. IT development often fails to accord sufficient priority to interoperability. By planning and prioritizing during the design phase of IT solutions, departments and agencies can enjoy community-wide benefits of interoperability while meeting individual mission mandates. Increasing interoperability and access to shared services and information improves mission success, minimizes complexity, and reduces duplication as well as ongoing sustainment requirements.

3.3 Leverage Collective Demand through Acquisition

An acquisition approach that integrates standards is essential for deploying interoperable technology solutions and shared services. Our ability to integrate systems and share information is stronger and more adaptable when government departments and agencies partner with one another and industry to identify and reuse the best solutions already at the government's disposal and to develop standards-based technologies that support multiple missions and communities. Stakeholders are encouraged to work with industry to develop and acquire tools and technologies leveraging information sharing and safeguarding standards. Federal acquisition policies, including grant policies, should facilitate and reward collaboration between departments and agencies resulting in reuse of existing services and encouraging development of enterprise-wide acquisition priorities. Aligning acquisition requirements should not only support interoperable technology acquisition, but also should lower incremental costs to departments and agencies with fewer acquisitions and reduced processing costs.

4. Strengthen Information Safeguarding through Structural Reform, Policy, and Technical Solutions

4.1 Reform Structures and Policy

Recent information breaches and disclosures highlight vulnerabilities in the protection of sensitive and classified information. Continued implementation of structural reform and standardized policies, however, will strengthen oversight as well as align security best practices.

The risk of unauthorized disclosure and misuse of information originates from insider threats and external intrusions; structural reforms must address both. The ability to safeguard information depends on implementing and strengthening policies and procedures that enable network monitoring and detection of anomalous behavior to identify insider threats and intrusions. Existing coordination bodies sustain the focus on information safeguarding and jointly own responsibility for developing effective technical policies and standards for coordinating government-wide implementation, conducting independent compliance assessments, and holding senior-level officials accountable. Aggregating appropriate information from counterintelligence, security, information assurance, and human resource elements, across multiple networks and domains, in near-real time, enables the appropriate authorities to proactively reduce and address security breaches. Likewise, developing a coordinated enterprise capability to monitor the health of our networks and detect malicious access attempts requires a comprehensive understanding of how applications and services are used across networks and security domains. Policies and procedures should also address unintended release of information. Prevention, detection, and mitigation policies, paired with appropriate supporting technologies, help create the assurance and trust among partners to confidently share information.

4.2 Enhance Data-Level Controls, Automated Monitoring, and Cross-Classification Solutions

Technology also plays an important role in developing our safeguarding capabilities. Progress requires we move from network to data-level controls with application interoperability. Increasingly granular security controls will improve access to information regardless of where information flows and strengthen protection against unauthorized disclosure, dissemination, access, and modification of information. Automated continuous monitoring, paired with appropriate privacy protections, supports shared risk management and enables a near real-time picture of existing or emerging risks.

The focus of information safeguarding efforts in the past was primarily bound to systems and networks at specific classification levels. Departments and agencies, however, often identify the need to securely share information across systems regardless of classification. Technologies, capabilities, and services such as shared computing further accelerate the need for cross-classification sharing. Consequently, we need technologies, standards, and common processes to support this critical emerging requirement.

5. Protect Privacy, Civil Rights, and Civil Liberties through Consistency and Compliance

5.1 Increase Consistent Government-Wide Application of Protections

Privacy, civil rights, and civil liberties protections are integral to maintaining the public trust; this is a cornerstone of our information sharing and safeguarding efforts. Departments and agencies will need to adopt a consistent approach to the foundational privacy, civil rights, and civil liberties protections for information they hold, with appropriate provisions for mission-based flexibility in accordance with existing law and policy. This leverages governance bodies and existing procedures, to continually refine and establish necessary guidelines for appropriate protections of shared information, such as the *Information Sharing Environment Privacy Guidelines*. Cultivating a comprehensive and efficient approach to defining and implementing privacy, civil rights, and civil liberties protections in information sharing between both Federal and non-Federal partners sustains applicable legal, regulatory, and policy requirements, an imperative for protecting both national security and individual rights.

5.2 Build Protections into the Development of Information Sharing Operations

Protecting privacy, civil rights, and civil liberties is not the exclusive domain of legal counsel and subject matter experts. Legal and policy controls on the use and protection of information may be implemented through the policy process and integrated in technology. This warrants participation by and coordination with program managers, system architects and developers, information assurance personnel, and others in program and system design. Addressing privacy, civil rights, and civil liberties early in the planning of any new initiative (or in the redesign of existing systems and processes) allows these information protections to be considered, built-in, managed, and monitored enterprise-wide.

5.3 Promote Accountability and Compliance Mechanisms

Ensuring compliance through oversight, performance management, and accountability with proper enforcement mechanisms is as critical as identifying the protections themselves. Each department and agency currently monitors and reports on the rigor of its privacy, civil rights, and civil liberties protections using appropriate compliance documentation and performance management techniques. Monitoring and measuring compliance verification mechanisms for accountability assists mission partners in identifying and addressing vulnerabilities, and in validating they are actively and systematically refining protections for individual rights. As we transition to an enterprise-wide approach, protections must be continuously reinforced and assessed, including monitoring of access and use controls, analysis of audit and usage information, and regular and systematic compliance reviews.

Privacy, civil rights, and civil liberties performance and compliance must evolve along with information sharing needs and methods. Going forward, this enterprise-wide model should include implementing technological means of reviewing and enforcing privacy, civil rights, and civil liberties protections, requirements, and policies.

V. Way Forward

As stated in the *National Security Strategy*, "collaboration across the government—and with our partners at the state, local, and tribal levels of government, in industry, and abroad—must guide our actions." This *Strategy* serves as a guide for balancing collective efforts to promote responsible sharing and safeguarding in support of national security and to enhance the safety of the American people. Together, we can reach beyond legacy information sharing protocols and embed in our missions and cultures the assurance decisions are better informed when supported by all relevant information. This also requires, however, a balanced commitment to appropriately safeguard information, its sources, and collection methods, while also respecting legal and policy restrictions on use. Success depends upon the collective ability to achieve equilibrium between sharing and safeguarding, build on past successes, and continue the maturation of the Information Sharing Environment.

An integrated implementation plan will be developed to provide a coordinated and sustainable approach to accomplish the goals and realize the vision of this *Strategy*. This plan will focus on achieving priority objectives, sequence stakeholder actions across a five-year horizon, include performance measures and milestones, and designate lead departments and agencies. The implementation plan will integrate annual programmatic and implementation guidance and synchronize with the Federal budget cycle to allow adjustments to actions and deliverables based on annual performance assessments, changing priorities, and resource allocations. Implementation planning will involve all departments and agencies that support national security and safety, led by the White House, leveraging the strategic resourcing processes of the Office of Management and Budget, and managed by departments, agencies, and executive agents, as appropriate, based on mission relevance and existing authorities.

Priority Objectives

Top Five

The following objectives capture the highest five priorities of the Administration in achieving the information sharing and safeguarding goals of this *Strategy*.

1. Align information sharing and safeguarding governance to foster better decisionmaking, performance, accountability, and implementation of the *Strategy's* goals.

2. Develop guidelines for information sharing and safeguarding agreements to address common requirements, including privacy, civil rights, and civil liberties, while still allowing flexibility to meet mission needs.

3. Adopt metadata standards to facilitate federated discovery, access, correlation, and monitoring across Federal networks and security domains.

4. Extend and implement the FICAM Roadmap across all security domains.

5. Implement removable media policies, processes and controls; provide timely audit capabilities of assets, vulnerabilities, and threats; establish programs, processes and techniques to deter,

detect and disrupt insider threats; and share the management of risks, to enhance unclassified and classified information safeguarding efforts.

Additional Priority Objectives

The remaining objectives represent additional priority activities for departments, agencies, and other stakeholders to advance the goals of this *Strategy*.

6. Define and adopt baseline capabilities and common requirements to enable data, service, and network interoperability.

7. Provide information sharing, safeguarding, and handling training to appropriate stakeholders using a common curriculum tailored to promote consistent, yet flexible, and trusted processes.

8. Define and implement common processes and standards to support automated policy-based discovery and access decisions.

9. Establish information sharing processes and sector specific protocols, with private sector partners, to improve information quality and timeliness and secure the nation's infrastructure.

10. Develop a reference architecture to support a consistent approach to data discovery and correlation across disparate datasets.

11. Implement the recommendations and activities of the Federal IT Shared Services Strategy among appropriate stakeholders to facilitate adoption of shared services.

12. Refine standards certification and conformance processes enabling standards-based acquisition among departments and agencies, standards bodies, and vendors to promote interoperable products and services.

13. Promote adherence to existing interagency processes to coordinate information sharing initiatives with foreign partners, as well as adopt and apply necessary guidelines, consistent with statutory authorities and Presidential policy to ensure consistency when sharing and safeguarding information.

14. Create a common process across all levels of government for Requests for Information, Alerts, Warnings, and Notifications to enable timely receipt and dissemination of information and appropriate response.

15. Complete the implementation of the NSI programs in the National Network of Fusion Centers and Federal entities while expanding training and outreach beyond law enforcement to the rest of the public safety community.

16. Achieve the four Critical Operational Capabilities, four Enabling Capabilities, and other prioritized objectives, across the National Network of Fusion Centers to enable effective and lawful execution of their role as a focal point within the state and local environment for the receipt, analysis, gathering and sharing of threat-related information.

National security stakeholders across the government, guided by our shared Principles, can now act in concert to accomplish these priority objectives and build implementation plans to realize the goals of this *Strategy*. As we execute the *Strategy* together, we will harness our collective resolve to treat information as a national asset, make it discoverable and retrievable by all authorized users, and arm those charged with preserving the security of our nation with all information available to drive decisions that protect our country and its people. Only as we work together, hold ourselves accountable, and take concerted ownership of advancing our goals, will we achieve the success our country rightfully demands and fully deserves.